W9-CZY-199

DATE DUE

MAR 1 5 2007		
JAN 0 2 2007	APR 1 0 2014	
FEB 2 3 2008	4/17/14	
MAR 2 4 2008	JAN 3 1 2015	
FEB 1 9 2009		
AUG 0 6 2010		
MAR 2 7 2010		
JUL 0 2 2011		
DEC 2 7 2011		
DEC 2 7 2011		
APR 25 2013		

HIGHSMITH 45230

Frederick Douglass

A Photo-Illustrated Biography
by Margo McLoone

Reading Consultant:
Dr. Gail Lowe
Anacostia Museum

Bridgestone Books
an Imprint of Capstone Press

Facts about Frederick Douglass
- Frederick Douglass was famous for speaking out against slavery.
- He was a slave whose English friends bought his freedom for $700.
- He took the name Douglass from a character in a book.
- He advised President Abraham Lincoln.

Bridgestone Books are published by Capstone Press • 818 North Willow Street, Mankato, Minnesota 56001
Copyright © 1997 by Capstone Press • All rights reserved • Printed in the United States of America

Library of Congress Cataloging-in-Publication Data
McLoone, Margo
    Frederick Douglass/by Margo McLoone
    p. cm.--(Read and discover photo-illustrated biographies)
    Includes bibliographical references and index.
    Summary: A brief biography of the man who escaped life as a slave in 1838 and became a great anti-slavery orator and advisor to president Abraham Lincoln.
    ISBN 1-56065-517-8
    1. Frederick, Douglass 1817?-1895--Juvenile literature. 2. Abolitionists--United States--Biography--Juvenile literature. 3. Afro-American abolitionists biography--Juvenile literature. 4. Antislavery movements--United States--Juvenile literature. [1. Douglass, Frederick, 1817?-1895. 2. Abolitionists. 3. Afro-Americans--Biography].
    I. Title. II. Series.
E449.D75M39   1997
973.8'092
[B]--DC21

        96-37384
        CIP
        AC

Photo credits
Schomburg Center, cover, 4, 16, 18
Unicorn/John, Ward, 6
Bettmann, 8, 10, 12, 14, 20

Table of Contents

The Voice of Freedom

Frederick Douglass was born a slave. A slave is a person who is owned by someone else. He taught himself to read and write. Then he escaped to freedom. He was a famous abolitionist. An abolitionist writes and speaks out against slavery.

Frederick spoke to many large audiences. People could not believe that a slave could speak so well. He also wrote the story of his life. Thousands of people read his book. It was called *Narrative of the Life of Frederick Douglass.*

Frederick was a freedom fighter. He started a newspaper for slaves. The newspaper was called the *North Star.* It printed poems and stories by African Americans. The newspaper reported on the fight against slavery.

Frederick wrote and spoke out against slavery.

Born a Slave

Frederick Augustus Washington Bailey was born in Tuckahoe, Maryland, in 1818. He was taken away from his mother, Harriet, at birth.

Frederick went to live with his grandmother. They lived in a small cabin on a plantation. A plantation is a large farm. Frederick's mother would sneak away from her plantation to visit him. At six years old, Frederick went to work in the fields. He worked all day. His only meal was a bowl of mush. Mush is boiled cornmeal. He slept on a dirt floor with other children.

Frederick's mother died when he was seven. Frederick was not allowed to go to her funeral.

Frederick lived in a small cabin similar to this with his grandmother.

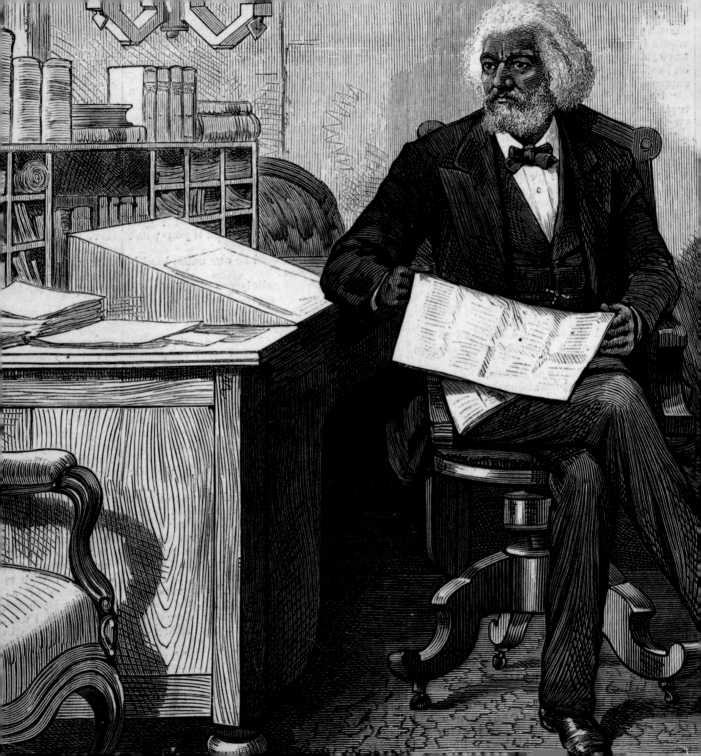

Learning to Read and Write

When he was about eight, Frederick was sent to Baltimore, Maryland. He was a gift for his owner's young nephew, Tommy Auld.

Frederick was more comfortable at the Auld house. He was given food and warm clothing. He discovered books. Frederick asked Tommy's mother to teach him how to read. She started to teach him, but Mr. Auld stopped her. He said that slaves should not read.

In secret, Frederick taught himself how to read. He asked neighborhood boys to teach him to write. Soon Frederick could read and write. He read newspapers. He learned about people who thought slavery was wrong.

Frederick taught himself to read.

Escape from Slavery

When Frederick grew older, he was sent back to the plantation. He worked long days in the fields. Frederick was mistreated. He was often beaten and did not get much food. He hated the life of slavery.

Frederick had a strong will. A master at the plantation tried to break Frederick's will. Frederick fought back.

Frederick was too much trouble. He was sent back to Baltimore. He tried to run away, but he was caught. He was put in jail. There, he planned his escape.

Frederick escaped by boarding a train for New York. He dressed up like a sailor. He carried a free slave's papers. He changed his name to Douglass. He was afraid of being caught.

Frederick hated slavery, and he tried to run away.

Marriage and Family

Frederick met Anna Murray in Baltimore. She was a free woman who worked as a maid. She joined him in New York after his escape. In 1838, they were married and left New York.

They moved to New Bedford, Massachusetts. There they were safe from slave catchers. Slave catchers were people hired to find runaway slaves. Frederick worked at the shipyards in a busy seaport.

In 1839, their first child Rosetta was born. She was followed by four other children. They were Lewis, Charles, young Frederick, and a sister, Annie. Annie was young when she died.

In 1838, Frederick met and married Anna Murray.

Powerful Speaker

In 1841, Frederick went to his first meeting against slavery. People were surprised to see a runaway slave at the meeting. Someone asked him to talk about being a slave.

Frederick told his story. He spoke in a deep voice. He spoke about his hatred for slavery. The audience of 500 people was shocked by his speech.

Frederick became known as a great speaker and writer. He was paid to tour and speak out against slavery. He wrote a book about his life. Thousands of people read his autobiography.

Frederick became too famous to be safe. He moved to England. His English friends bought his freedom for $700.

Frederick became known as a great speaker and writer.

The Civil War

In 1847, Frederick returned to the United States. Frederick and his family lived in Rochester, New York. He began publishing a newspaper that spoke out against slavery. It was called the *North Star*. In 1861, war broke out. The Northern states fought the Southern states. Slavery was one of the reasons for the war.

Frederick said African Americans should fight in the war against slavery. His three sons joined the Northern army. Frederick met with President Abraham Lincoln to talk about black soldiers and runaway slaves.

In 1863, President Lincoln signed the Emancipation Proclamation. This was a written order that freed all slaves.

Frederick published a newspaper that spoke out against slavery.

Important Government Jobs

After the war, Frederick worked to win the right for African Americans to vote. In 1872, he moved to Washington, D.C. In 1877, he became the United States marshal for Washington, D.C. A marshal is someone who keeps peace in a community. It was the highest government position held by an African American.

Anna died in 1882 after a long illness. In 1884, Frederick married Helen Pitts. Together, they worked to give women the right to vote.

In 1889, Frederick became the U. S. minister to Haiti. After two years in Haiti, he became sick and returned home.

Helen Pitts, sitting on the right, married Frederick in 1884.

Freedom Fighter

Frederick Douglass devoted his life to fighting against slavery. He gave speeches and wrote articles. He helped runaway slaves escape to freedom. He fought for the rights of all people.

On February 20, 1895, Frederick Douglass died of a heart attack at his home in Washington, D.C. He was 77 years old.

Frederick was a great speaker and leader. Thousands of people attended his funeral. He was buried in Rochester, New York. This was where he had spent most of his life.

On February 20, 1895, Frederick died of a heart attack at his home in Washington, D.C.

Words from Frederick Douglass

"Every tone (of the songs of the slaves) was a testimony against slavery, and a prayer to God for deliverance from chains."

From his autobiography, *Narrative of the Life of Frederick Douglass*, 1845.

"No man can put a chain about the ankle of his fellow man without at last finding the other end fastened about his own neck."

Speech at a civil rights meeting, Washington, D.C., October 22, 1883.

Important Dates in Frederick Douglass' Life

1818—Born in Tuckahoe, Maryland

1825—Sent to Baltimore, Maryland, as a slave

1838—Escapes to freedom

1838—Marries Anna Murray

1841—Delivers his first speech against slavery

1845—Publishes his autobiography

1845—Flees to England where friends buy his freedom

1847—Returns to Rochester, New York

1847—Starts a newspaper called the *North Star*

1861—Civil War begins; Douglass recruits black soldiers

1863—Emancipation Proclamation frees all slaves

1872—Moves to Washington, D.C.

1877—Becomes the marshal of Washington, D.C.

1889—Becomes the U. S. minister to Haiti

1895—Dies in Washington, D.C.

Words to Know

abolitionist (ab-uh-LISH-uh-nist)—a person who works toward ending slavery.

mush (MUHSH)— boiled cornmeal

plantation (plan-TAY-shuhn)—a large farm

Emancipation Proclamation (i-man-si-PAY-shun pruh-kla-MAY-shun)—a written order given by president Abraham Lincoln to free all slaves in 1863

slave catcher (SLAYV KA-chur)—a person who was hired to catch runaway slaves

Read More

Bennett, Evelyn. *Frederick Douglass and the War Against Slavery*. Brookfield, Conn.: Millbrook Press, 1993.

Huggins, Nathan Irvin. *Slave and Citizen: The Life of Frederick Douglass*. Boston: Little Brown, 1980.

McKissack, Patricia and Frederick McKissack. *Frederick Douglass: The Black Lion*. Chicago: Children's Press, 1987.

McKissack, Patricia and Frederick McKissack. *Frederick Douglass: LeaderAgainst Slavery*. Hillside, N.J.: Enslow Publishers, 1991.

Useful Addresses

Frederick Douglass National Historic Site
14th & "W" Street SE
Washington, DC 20020

Afro-American Resource Center
P.O. Box 746
Howard University
Washington, DC 20005

Internet Sites

Frederick Douglass African-American Historical Figure
http://www.webcom.com/~bright/source/fdougla.html
The Frederick Douglass Museum & Cultural Center
http://www.ggw.org/freenet/f/fdm/index.html

Index